Our *Thoughtful* Readers

This book is dedicated to our thoughtful readers—who obviously love color as much as we do!

In this book, the third in the *Copic Coloring Guide* series, we endeavor to cover a topic that is near and dear to our hearts—coloring people.

Whether you enjoy realistic, vintage, cute or whimsical, the popularity of "people" images is unprecedented. There are literally thousands of images available just begging to be colored.

In the following pages you will find not only photo tutorials stepping you through the most popular methods of coloring skin and hair and a variety of clothing, but also the theory that explains the why behind those techniques.

We, again, want to give you the coloring basics, the stepping stones to your success, and have you adapt and apply them to your own works. To that end, we have included a CD that contains each of the hand-drawn images used in the tutorial section along with blank charts for recording skin tones, hair color combinations and favorite patterns and textures.

We hope you embrace this book as much as the previous ones and that it finds a home in your crafting library.

—Colleen and Marianne

Coloring
Faces

The face is the most important part of any image. It shows expression and feeling and conveys character.

Light It Up!

Before beginning to color an image it is necessary to identify the light source to determine where the light is coming from in the image.

Keep the images "facing" the light source.

Let's start this exercise by considering some common lighting scenarios. If a person is outside during the day, the light source is the sun. If a person is inside a home during the evening hours, the light source is most likely an overhead light or lamp. If a person is telling ghost stories around a campfire, the light source is probably the roaring fire.

The light from a source will illuminate the things around it and create areas of highlight and areas of shadow. It is important to understand where the light source is when coloring images, especially when faces are included, in order to create accurate and realistic highlights and shadows. Keep the following rules in mind to make the task easier.

Rule 1: Always highlight the most important part of the image by having the light shine directly on that aspect. On people images, the face is typically the focal point.

Rule 2: The image should always "face" the light source.

Notice how the young girl is sitting at an angle on the bench. Even though she is glancing down, her face is still facing left. Keeping Rule 2 in mind, place the light source in the upper left corner when coloring this image.

Rule 3: Areas that are closest to the light source are brightest and most highlighted.

Turn on a lamp. Hold your hand up to the light. The side of your hand that is closest to the light is bright and the side that is facing away from the lamp is dark or in shadow. Keep this concept in mind when coloring your images.

Seeing the Rules at Work

Look at the images on this page and apply the three previous rules about light source.

Notice on the top image how the front of her dress, the cover of the book, her face, and the front of her hat are all brightly lit. Notice too how the back of the hat, behind the book and the back of her dress are all in shadow. With the light source coming from the upper left, her face and the book become the focal point of the image.

Now notice the coloring on the image at the right. Same girl, sitting on the same bench and reading the same book, but it looks totally different because the light source has changed. In this image, the light source is coming from the upper right side of the image, behind her, highlighting her bow, the hat and the back of her head. Since her body and face are facing away from the light, they are thrown into shadow.

While this is not an incorrect light source, it does not convey that the girl and her book are most important.

The light source is coming from the upper right side.

Faces—Simple & Complex

When it comes to face images, there are many different styles on the market—from small and simple to largely complex and detailed. Some are cute and whimsical while others are more realistic. Whatever style you prefer, there are some easy tips and tricks to help color them well. If you have never attempted a large, fully detailed face before, it can be intimidating. We recommend starting with simple images and working up to more detailed ones.

Simple Faces

This little girl is similar to many images on the market today. She has a basic, round face shape with uncomplicated facial features. Since the image itself is simple, we want to keep the coloring simple too.

Notice that this image is only colored in two or three values. Any more and it would look too detailed. Keep it simple—a highlight (shown by the white), a mid tone (C1) and a shadow (C3).

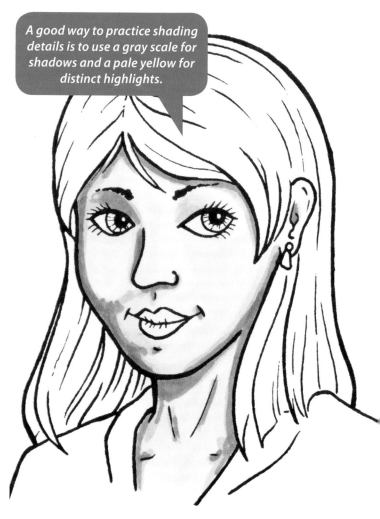

A good way to practice shading details is to use a gray scale for shadows and a pale yellow for distinct highlights.

Complex Faces

Here's an image that is larger, more realistic and much more detailed. It calls for more values and more attention to detail to create a cohesive look.

This image is shown with five distinct values—Y11 for highlights, white for light areas, C1 for light shading, C3 for darker shading and C5 for darkest shadows.

Focus on Features

When coloring complex faces, it is important to pay attention to the features as they can make or break a composition.

The Eyes Have It

People say the eyes are the windows to the soul. Here are a few tips to help capture the "essence" of the character through the eyes.

The iris is not a flat disk of color; it curves with the eyeball. To portray this, it is important to have a variation of shade. The iris is typically darker near the top and bottom where it meets the eyelids and/or near the corner of the eye when looking toward the side.

The eyeball is round. While the eyeball is typically left uncolored, define its shape by adding a touch of gray or lavender to create a shadow near the edges and along the upper eyelid.

Everyone wants that sparkle in his or her eyes. Create it by using a tiny dot of Opaque White to add a bright highlight to the iris. ***Note:*** *There is already a tiny highlight in the pupil of this image. Feel free to add another (larger) highlight to the lightest part of the iris.*

Luscious Lips

A pretty pout is easy if you remember one thing—the bottom lip is usually fuller than the top lip and therefore sticks out more. Because it sticks out from the face, it catches more light and should be highlighted. Notice that the corners of the lips and where the lips meet and recede are therefore darkest.

The Surface of the Face

A face is not flat. It's a basic sphere, curving away from the viewer above the forehead, below the chin and along the ears. There are ridges and valleys that jut out to catch the light or sink in to create shadows. It is important to think of a face with volume and to understand how the different features "sit" on its surface.

Eyes

The eyes sit back in the head a bit. There is a brow bone that protrudes above the eye and a cheekbone that slopes out underneath.

Nose

The nose is probably the most feared facial feature, but it is actually fairly simple. Most detailed drawings will give you a hint of nose shape and placement. It is up to you to fill in what isn't there. The easiest thing to remember about the nose is that it sticks out from the face and will block light. The bridge of the nose will be the brightest, while the sides of the nose will have a bit of shading. The side closest to the light source will have subtle shading that flows down from the brow bone. The side furthest from the light source will have a darker cast shadow. The tip of the nose curves down and around, so there is slight shading along the edge of the tip. If the light is from above, there will also be a slight shadow under the nose.

Lips

These are pretty simple. They stick out from the face, catching the light, and therefore create subtle shadows.

Add shading to the areas under the brows, along the eyelid crease and along the underside corner of the eye.

Add a touch of shading at the corners of the lips, below the bottom lip and above the chin, and in the small crease above the center of the top lip.

Cheeks

Some images have very prominent cheekbones and others are less defined. If the image has prominent cheekbones, they will stick out from the face catching a bit of light and creating highlights. They may also create slight areas of shadow along the jawbone below the cheeks.

Coloring
Skin

"What is a good skin-color combination?"
It's a frequently asked question and unfortunately,
there's no simple answer. What are you coloring?
Is it a young or old character? What size is the image?
What sort of tone are you looking to portray?

You're How Old?

Everyone wants to have younger-looking skin. We spend hundreds of dollars on creams, masks, treatments and ointments. What does younger skin look like and why is it so attractive? It is important to understand that the appearance of our skin changes as we age, and making an age-appropriate color choice is very important.

Young Skin

Young skin is typically bright, smooth and moist. Babies and young children often have a peach or pinkish "glow" that is considered youthful.

Look at the toddler in the image below. His skin is very light and has a peach-color base. Also notice how smooth the skin is. This is because baby fat keeps his skin plump and wrinkle free.

YR000, E11, E13, BV11

Keep shading to a minimum as a toddler's skin is smooth and tight and deep shadows from wrinkles or creases just aren't visible.

When coloring images of babies or young children, make sure to start with a pink or peach base tone. Here YR000 is used to create a youthful glow. Even if the child is of a darker ethnicity, begin by coloring your image in the same manner.

Do not over-blend with the lighter colors as this will create a splotchy, mottled look that isn't appropriate for smooth, youthful skin.

Young Adult Skin

As we age, we lose the "glow" we associate with youth. This comes from a combination of stress, impurities, environmental exposure and the natural loss of collagen that keeps our skin firm and elastic.

Take a look at the young woman in the next photo. While her skin is still fairly smooth and wrinkle free, she is no longer as pink as the toddler.

E50, E30, E21, E24, BV02

She still has a bit of a glow, but it is more golden brown in tone. Her face has more distinct shadows than the child, but her skin is still fairly smooth.

Older Adult Skin

Aging eventually causes some very drastic changes in our skin. Old skin looks wrinkled, saggy, thin and mottled. This is mostly caused by the loss of elasticity and prolonged exposure to the elements.

The elderly man in the image below has probably spent years on the water, fishing for his next big catch.

E000, E42, E70, E71, E44, E04, E53, B21, BV31

Notice that his skin appears thin. There is a yellow undertone that is sallow instead of youthful. E000 and E42 have been used to create this sallow look. The shadows are very prominent due to the deep creases and wrinkles. The shading is done in cool tones adding to his ashy complexion. Elderly skin is often mottled and blotchy, so going over the darker shadows with the lighter color will help create that splotchy look; just make sure to leave the shadows dark.

Coloring for Size

Now that we've answered the question of age—let's talk size. We've already discussed a bit about the difference between simple and complex images, and in the previous books in this series we explained that more shades equal more contrast which, in turn, equals more interest. Let's take the discussion a bit further and talk about color choice in relation to size.

Two-Color Blends for Small Spaces

In this schoolboy image, the face is relatively tiny compared to the image as a whole—approximately ½ inch. Trying to fit multiple shades into the tiny area will only muddle the features.

Here E30 and E21 have been used. You won't be able to create the dramatic contrast of using multiple shades, but you will keep the facial features clear and visible and the light source identifiable.

For tiny images, create subtle shading with just two colors.

Three Color Blends for Mid-Size Spaces

Most people like to use three-shade color combos when coloring skin. If the image allows, this is a definite improvement over just two shades.

This image is very similar in size to many popular images on the market today. The face measures just over 1 inch and has simple, but recognizable features.

Images this size allow for more shades and therefore allow the colorist to create more contrast. This image uses E50, E21 and E34 to create a light skin tone with subtle shading and darker cast shadows. Notice that it is visually more interesting than the schoolboy's face.

Four or More Color Blends for Larger Spaces

This image is quite large at 2½–3 inches and includes fully formed facial features and details. Images like this beg for multiple-shade color combinations.

While it may seem intimidating at first, coloring a large image is not much different than coloring smaller images—it just uses more ink!

Here, a base of E50 is quickly enhanced with E11, E33, E04, E70 and BV02. Notice the stark contrast achievable by using so many different shades. Remember, contrast creates interest!

For larger images, use more colors to create shading.

Color Combinations

The Basics

Once you've taken age and size into consideration, begin choosing colors for the skin tone. There are no hard and fast rules for what colors should be used together. Stick with the basic blending families for smooth natural blends or experiment with a variety of colors and families to create your own favorite combos. Don't feel like you need to stick with the Earth color family. Reach for the YR's or the Y's or even the R's for a variety of looks.

Think about the Copic numbering system—the last number tells the shade of the color. Think about the colors you typically use for coloring skin. What is the darkest shade you use? 0? 1? Maybe 2? If you are courageous you might use a 3.

Guess what? You can do better! Most people are intimidated by coloring skin, and since the face is such an important focal point, they lean toward the side of caution and leave the skin tone too light. If the goal of your coloring is to be realistic, you need to not be afraid of the dark.

In our previous books, we discussed using colors ending in 6–9 to create shadows. While 7s, 8s and 9s are extremely dense shades, they can be used for shading and shadows for skin if used sparingly. Remember that the darker the base color, the darker the shadows.

A good way to practice creating darker skin tones is to "one up" the shade on your normal color combination. If your favorite skin combination is E0000, E00, E01, try adding E02 instead of E01. This will bump up the shade just slightly.

E0000, E00, E02

Once you feel comfortable with the look, jump "one up" again, adding another shade to the mix.

As you start to see your skin tones with more contrast and more realistic shading, you will quickly start expanding your skin-tone choices.

E0000, E00, E02, E04

Tips & Tricks

- *There is one very common mistake made when coloring skin: People tend to color too light. During our research we found that one of the most popular skin-color combos was E0000 and E00 with possibly a bit of E01.*

E0000, E00, E01

This is really, really light—like vampire light!

- *Don't over-blend. Gently blend shading but leave cast shadows crisp.*

- *The larger the image, the more colors used.*

- *Don't be afraid of the dark.*

- *Pay attention to the base color. It creates the tone.*

It's All About the Amount!

So you've been practicing coloring skin and are feeling more comfortable with darker colors. Here's something to consider when using those darker shades: The amount of each color you use will change the skin tone.

Take a look at the following images.

While both of these images use E00, E21 and E34 for the skin-color combination, they end up looking somewhat different. The first image has just a touch of E34 in the shadows and it is blended out fully with the E21, giving it a much lighter appearance. The second image has more E34 and it is only blended out slightly, creating a much darker skin tone.

Once you find a color combination you like, start playing with the amount of the darker shades to change up the look and give you a variety of skin tones.

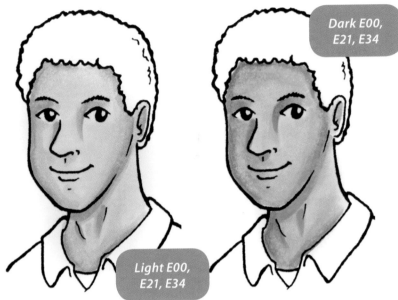

Dark E00, E21, E34

Light E00, E21, E34

Skin-Tone Chart

Print blank skin-tone charts from the included CD!

Experiment & Practice

Use a blank chart as the perfect place to try out different skin tones and play around with a variety of color combinations. Don't worry about getting the coloring and shading perfect—this is just a trial piece.

Print the chart onto the paper you typically use for Copic® coloring.

Pick a skin-color combination and color in one image. Write down the colors used on the line below the image.

Color in a second image using the same color combination with more or less of the darker shades. Try to get a variety of looks from the same group of colors.

Continue practicing and experimenting with different color combinations. Try two-, three- and four-color combos.

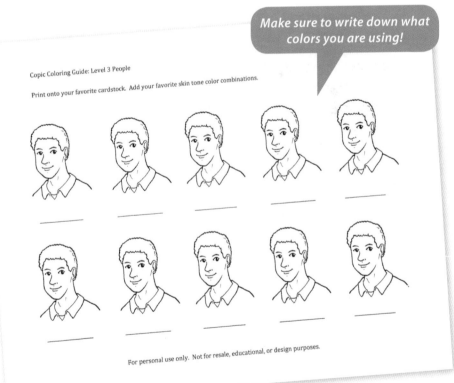

Make sure to write down what colors you are using!

Reference Chart

Once you have a number of favorite skin-color combinations, it's time to put them all together. This will be a reference chart, so try to be consistent in your placement of shading and shadows.

Here are two pages from my skin-tone reference charts. They are arranged from light to dark (left to right), each row being a different tone. The first row is peach/pink undertones; the second is brown and red tones. The third is olive tones and the last is gray and brown tones. Feel free to organize your charts as you wish and use as many as necessary.

Copic Coloring Guide: Level 3 People

Skin Tone Chart

Print onto your favorite cardstock. Add your favorite skin tone color combinations.

Ecooo/E01/E31   Ecooo/E01/E11/E04   Ecoo/E21/E34   Yeoo/E11/E21/E23   Ecooo/E01/E31/E25

E30/E21/E33/E15   E21/E34/E25   E11/E13/E15/E37   E21/E13/E25/E27   E11/E34/E17/E29

For personal use only. Not for resale, educational, or design purposes.

Skin Tone Chart

E50/E31/E04   E50/E53/E71/E04   E51/E31/E55/E74   E53/E55/E57   E31/E34/E37

E42/E44/E47   E43/E74/E77   E33/E44/E57   E35/E57/E77   E57/E59/E49
Final Blend w/ E55

For personal use only. Not for resale, educational, or design purposes.

Creating Ethnicities

I know, I know—you still want to know what color combinations to use for Caucasian skin, or African-American skin or Asian skin. There are no set rules here, but we do have a few tips to share about ethnicities.

Most of the E0 family is very peach and will give a pink or peach tone to the skin. Good for young children, pale Caucasian or sunburned skin.

The E2 family has a brown or golden tone perfect for tanned Caucasian skin or light Asian skin.

The E5 family is olive and works well for Mediterranean, Middle Eastern and Asian skin tones.

The E7 family is a rich cocoa brown and works well as shading for darker skin tones.

The E3 family is reddish and is good for Caucasian, Native American, Latino, African-American and Asian skin tones.

Tips & Tricks

- *When creating a variety of ethnicities in your skin tones, don't be stuck in the rules or blending families. Each color reacts differently when combined with other colors. To get proficient in creating realistic ethnic skin tones, you need to experiment and practice.*

The E4 family is a bit gray. It is often used in African-American or Middle Eastern skin tones.

E000
E00
E01
E02
E04

E21
E23
E25
E27
E29

E30
E31
E33
E34
E35
E37
E39

E40
E41
E42
E43
E44
E47
E49

E50
E51
E53
E55
E57
E59

E70
E71
E74
E77
E79

Complement It & Cool It!

In book 2 of the Copic Coloring Guide *series, we demonstrated how to add shading using a complementary color and how to cool down shadows. Those same rules can be applied to coloring realistic skin.*

Most skin is yellow or orange in tone. The complementary color to yellow is purple and the complementary color to orange is blue, therefore, a blue violet is the perfect color to add realistic shading to skin.

Blue violet also tends to be a cool color, effectively working to cool down those shadows.

Compare these images.

The first image is colored with a combination of E000, E11, E13 and E15. Notice the soft, warm glow in the skin. The shadows are visible, but don't contrast much.

Notice the subtle difference in the second image. The skin is colored with the same combination as the first image, with the addition of BV000 and BV11 in the shadows. It's noticeable, but not glaring. The shadows are cooled off and contrast nicely with the skin tones making the image a much more realistic representation.

Warm shading

Blend the purples in slightly to create shading or leave them crisp for cast shadows.

Cool shading

Tips & Tricks for Coloring Skin

- *When coloring skin, use the basic blending technique.*
- *For super smooth blends, go over the entire image with the lighter colors when blending.*
- *Avoid over blending and losing contrast.*
- *Avoid using the Colorless Blender when coloring skin as it will change the tone and give skin a splotchy appearance.*
- *Create smooth edges and soft shadows by keeping the layers wet.*
- *Create crisp edges and hard shadows by letting the ink dry between layers.*
- *Add dots of Opaque White to cheeks, eyes and/or lips to give a crisp, reflective highlight.*

You Make Me Blush

The final touch to coloring skin is adding blush. The first thing to consider is the image itself. Does it lend itself to the use of blush? Many of the cute, less-detailed images beg for rosy cheeks while larger, more-detailed images can do without. The direction of the face is also a consideration. Straight-on faces make for creating easy cheeks, while side views or profile images make adding cheeks more difficult.

Straight-On Image

Step 1: Color face as normal (E000, E21, E04).

Step 2: If you want crisp edges to your cheeks, let dry and then proceed to Step 3. If you want blended edges to your cheeks, proceed immediately to Step 3.

Step 3: Hold the marker vertically and quickly dab down onto the cardstock (E93).

The quicker and lighter you dab, the smaller and lighter the cheeks; the harder and slower you dab, the larger and darker the cheeks.

Complex or Side-View Image

Step 1: Color image as normal (E000, E21, E04).

Step 2: While skin tones are still wet, brush cheek color onto cheek area using a flicking motion that starts from the shaded area. Typically flick from ear toward nose (E93).

Step 3: Use a lighter skin color and flick slightly over blush color to blend (E00).

Coloring *Hair*

Hair—it comes in thousands of styles, textures and colors. That's what makes it one of our most distinguishable and recognizable characteristics.

Basic Guidelines for Lighting, Shading & Technique

Guideline 1: Halos

Everyone has a halo. The "ring" of highlights that circle the head creates a halo. Take a look in the mirror or peek at your neighbor. Notice the halo?

Because most lighting comes from above, light will reflect off of the hair along a curved line around the upper part of the head. To decide where to add highlights, identify where the halo would be.

Notice the boy's head is turned slightly and bent down. The halo always curves around the upper portion of the head. Even if the head is tilted or turned, the halo will be near the top of the image.

Guideline 2: Crown Down, Tips Up

Hair grows from the crown of the head and flows down following the shape of the head. Always color in the direction of the hair growth. Anything different will look unnatural. Since hair grows from the crown down, the crown will be the darkest area on the head. We know that the halo area will be the lightest highlights, so that leaves us with the tips. The rule is—crown down, tips up—always coloring toward the halo.

Notice the arrows in the picture to the left. The hair is colored from the crown down and the tips up, leaving the middle "halo" area light.

Guideline 3: Use the Flick

We want the look of texture in our hair, so we use the flicking motion to apply ink. **Note:** *Check out book 1 of the* Copic Coloring Guide *series for a tutorial on flicking.* Flick from the crown down toward the halo, and flick from the tips up toward the halo.

Notice that the flick always starts in the same spot. Overlapping the beginning of each flick will naturally create a darker area near the crown and the tip. Vary the length of each flick.

Guideline 4: Hide in the Shadows

The underside of the hair, often shown along the neck and shoulders, will be darker since it gets less light.

On the sample image shown here, notice how the hair under her right cheek is slightly darker since her face blocks some of the light. If hair is tucked behind an ear or clipped in a barrette or bow, it will be darker where it is bunched or pulled together.

E41, E43, E44, W5

Y11, Y32, Y26, Y28, BV02

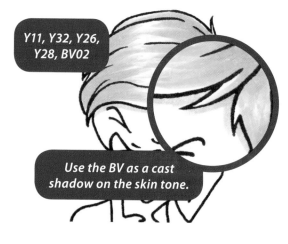

Use the BV as a cast shadow on the skin tone.

Guideline 5: Cast a Shadow

Hair that overlays the face and will cast a shadow on the face and possibly on the neck or shoulders. Cast shadows are subtle but crisp as demonstrated on the image shown here.

Simple Vs. Complex Hair

Coloring hair can be simple or it can be complex. Each requires a different approach.

Simple Hair

Let's step through coloring simple hair. Remember the basic guidelines from the previous section.

Step 1: Base hair with lightest color (E11).

Step 2: Add flicks of medium color (E23). Remember to flick from the crown down toward the halo and up from the tips toward the halo.

Step 3: Add flicks of darkest color (E39).

Do NOT blend. Leave the flicks visible to create texture for the hair.

Notice that the left side and the right side sections are done separately.

Complex Hair

Because complex hair is often wavy or curly, the halo isn't always as clear to define as on simple hair shapes. Notice that the hair sample here is separated into sections. With complex hair, think about each section and decide where it curves out toward the light (highlighted) and where it curves under or behind other sections (shadows).

Step 1: Color each section with lightest color (E11). You can base the entire hair area all at once instead of doing it strand by strand. You may find it helpful to color one section at a time to help plan and visualize the rest of the steps.

Step 2: Begin adding medium color (E23) to each section. Flick from the top of the section down and the tip of the section up. Leave any areas that curve away from the head or the center of the section light.

Step 3: Add darkest color (E39) to each section. Flick from the top of the section down and the tip up toward the highlight area.

> *Do not blend hair! Keep flicks visible to show texture.*

> *As darker colors are added, flicks become thinner and shorter.*

Tips & Tricks

- *Highlights in hair are not white. Base the entire image with the lightest color to give highlights depth.*

> *Complex hair colored using the "simple" method. Notice how unnatural the highlights look in the formal halo.*

Hair Style

Hair is not only simple or complex, but also comes in all sorts of styles and textures! Each one is approached differently. Keep the general guidelines in mind to help you create realistic-looking locks.

Straight Hair

Straight hair is probably the easiest to color and was demonstrated earlier with the simple hair tutorial. Here we've thrown in some bows to give you a bit of a challenge.

Step 1: Identify the halo.

Since this image has bows that are right in the area of the normal highlight and pull the hair together, create two separate areas of highlight. **Note:** *Remember, areas that are pulled together are darker.* This image would have two individual halos to illuminate the

highlights, one closer to the crown and one farther away.

Step 2: Base hair with lightest color (Y23).

Step 3: Add flicks of medium color (YR24). Notice the two areas of highlight.

Step 4: Add flicks of darkest color (YR27). Do not blend.

Wavy Hair

Wavy hair is sometimes drawn in a simple form (as shown) or in separate sections like the complex sample from the earlier section. When drawn in separate sections, color as demonstrated previously.

Wavy hair in simple form can be intimidating because the direction of the hair growth can change within a section. Follow these steps to easily color wavy hair in simple form.

Step 1: Identify direction of hair growth and areas of highlight.

Notice the dips and bulges. These are clues to highlight placement.

Step 2: Base the entire hair area with lightest color (YR21).

Step 3: Add flicks of medium color (E15) from crown to highlight area and tips to highlight area. Be aware that the ribbons pull the hair together and create a second area of highlight. Notice the flicks are a bit more wiggly and unstructured than in the straight hair.

Step 4: Add flicks of dark color (E18).

Many people find this style of hair difficult to color because it is looser and more random. Relax; don't get caught up in the structure of straight hair. Wavy hair by nature is more random.

Curly Hair

Curly hair has great volume, great texture and great character. It also has its own distinct technique for coloring.

Step 1: Base hair area with lightest color (E23).

Step 2: Add medium color by making loose scribbles (E27).

Step 3: Add dark color by making loose scribbles (E49).

Tips & Tricks

- *Another option for coloring curly hair is to add dots of the medium and dark color instead of scribbles. The dots allow for a bit more control in placement of shades.*

Notice that the scribbles are random and do not cover all of the light areas.

Color Combinations

Coming up with color combinations for hair is probably one of the most exciting challenges about coloring people. There are literally thousands of hair colors, and with the number of color choices in the Copic line, you will never run out of options for combinations.

While you can use virtually any color combination to color hair, it is important to understand that the very first color you use has a large impact on the final outcome. We call this the undertone.

Let's take a look at two images with hair colored in the same color combination, but with a different base color.

Both images are colored with E21, E33 and E57. The first photo has a base of Y23, giving it a slightly golden-brown tone. This really brightens up the highlight. The second image has a base of R20, giving it a red tone—the end result being a richer, darker brown hair color.

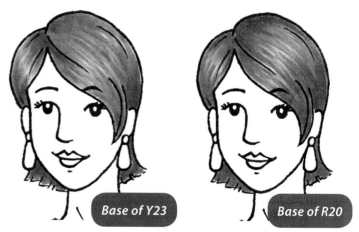

Base of Y23

Base of R20

Experiment with various base colors to create different undertones for your favorite color combinations.

Hair Color Chart

Copic Coloring Guide: Level 3 People
Print onto your favorite cardstock. Add your favorite hair color combinations.

Experiment & Practice

We have included a blank hair color chart on the CD for you to print for your personal use. Print the chart on your favorite cardstock. Use this as a way to practice and experiment with color combinations. Once you have compiled a list of favorites, print off a chart and fill it in to use as a reference. Make sure to write down what colors you use.

Reference Charts

Here are some samples from my own reference charts. The first page includes hair colors that range from pale blond to dark brown and the second from red to black.

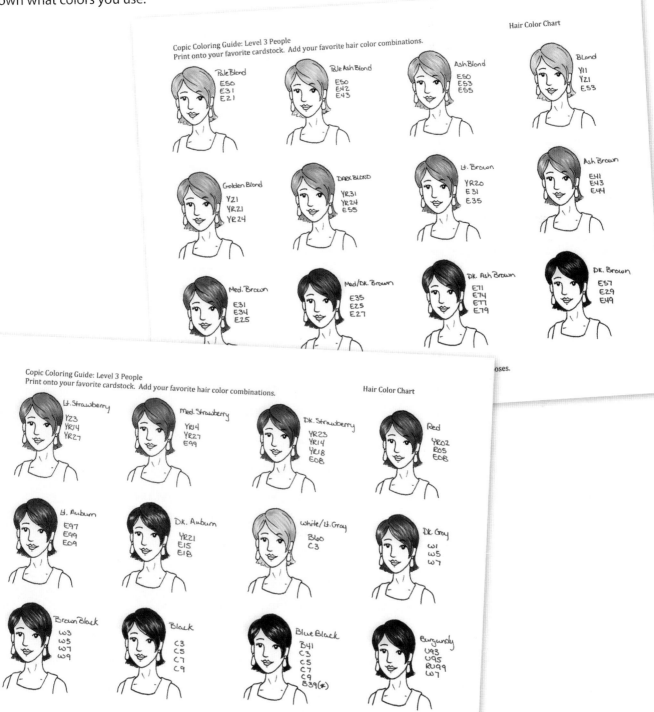

Coloring
Fabric &
Clothing

Coloring clothing realistically can be as challenging as coloring faces and hair. There are so many textures, patterns and fabrics, and portraying how they fit and move on a body is a study in itself.

Draping: Pleats & Folds

When looking at clothing that hangs loosely from the body, you will notice that the way it hangs varies depending on the type of fabric. Heavy, stiff material will have straight, possibly crisp pleats while light, airy material will have soft, flowing folds. There are different techniques to help illustrate these different types of draping.

Pleats

Pleats are crisp folds made in fabric that is typically heavy and stiff. The pleats are sharp and there is definite depth to certain areas.

Step 1: Base the whole skirt in the lightest color (V20).

Step 2: Add shading to the skirt with the medium color (V22). The light is coming from the upper right in this image, so the shading on the skirt will be on the left side.

Step 3: Deepen shading by adding the darkest color and blending smoothly.

Step 4: Begin adding shadows with dark color (V25).

> *Place shadows in each of the sections folded under and along the bottom of the books and hands.*

Step 5: Darken the shadows with a darker color (V28).

> *Notice the slight shadow at the left edge of each upper section of cloth.*

Folds

Fabric folds are much harder to articulate, both in words and in illustration. Folds often occur when material is loose and drapes away from the body. Most people identify folds with dresses and wide skirts, but they can also appear on things like sleeves on a loose sweater or the legs of trousers that are a bit too long.

There are two keys to coloring folds effectively. One is to concentrate on shading, blending smoothly into shadowed areas instead of having crisp definition, and the other is always coloring in the direction of the wrinkles. ***Note:*** *Four different shades will be used to complete this image. They will be referenced as light, mid-light, mid-dark and dark.*

Step 1: Identify any areas that lend themselves to fabric folds. In this image, the lines in the skirt give hints as to where the fabric is folding or rippling.

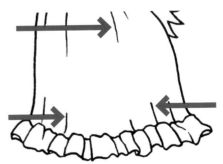

Step 2: Using the mid-light color (R83), sketch in lines along fold areas.

Notice that the colored lines are next to, not on top of, each of the image lines. To do this effectively, decide on a light source first. Here it is coming from straight on, so the folds on the left side of the image have the inked line to the left of the image lines, while the folds on the right side of the image have the inked line to the right side of the image lines.

Step 3: Using the light color (R81), fill in the image. Leave the area opposite the shaded side white.

This is just the planning stage and is imperative in helping to set up highlighted areas.

Step 4: Using the mid-dark color (R85), expand the shading of the folds. Go over the areas that were identified as shading areas in Step 2, making them both longer

and wider. Notice the additional shaded fold near the bottom of the center of the skirt.

Step 5: Using the mid-light and light colors (R83, R81), blend slightly. Make sure to leave the highlight areas white.

Step 6: Repeat Steps 4 and 5. It's all about back and forth with this technique.

Add more color, getting wider and longer each time. Blend it out. Repeat. Do this as many times as necessary to fully identify the folds. Each time, tighten up the areas of highlight until they are small and narrow.

Step 7: Using the darkest color (R89), add depth to the areas of darkest shading.

This step will really bring out the intensity of the folds.

Step 8: Using the mid-dark shade (R85), gently blend. Continue blending with the lighter colors (R83, R81) as you move toward the highlight areas. In this last step, go over the white highlight areas with the lightest shade (R81) just once to soften the highlights.

Types of Fabric

From the nappy feel of knit to the cool slide of silk, fabrics have different looks and very distinct feels. It's a fun challenge to try to make our colored fabrics look like a specific type. Here are tutorials for four of the most popular fabric types.

Silk & Satin

The shimmer and sheen of silk and satin are unmistakable. It's important to capture that "glow" in your coloring. Bright highlights with soft blending are a must. Here's how:

Step 1: Base dress with lightest color (C1).

Step 2: Add mid-light color (C3) to start shading.

Step 3: Add mid-dark color (C5) to continue deepening shading.

Step 4: Add dark color (C7) to deepest shadows.

Step 5: Blend colors together.

Step 6: Add darkest color (C9) to accent shading and blend out to soften edges.

Cotton

Cotton is typically soft and cozy—with a little bit of texture. Blends will be gradual and highlights subtle.

Step 1: Base the entire sweater with the lightest color (BG53).

Step 2: Add in shading with the medium color (BG57). Blend slightly.

Don't be afraid to go dark, as the texture will lighten up the whole image.

Step 3: Add final shading and cast shadows with darkest color (BG78).

Step 4: Let dry completely.

Step 5: Lightly dampen a washcloth or textured rag with Colorless Blender solution. Gently apply to colored sweater area and hold for a few seconds. Do not press or squeeze. Lift the cloth to reveal the texture.

Patent Leather, Rubber & Plastic

There's just something special about these fabric surfaces. It's not so much about the coloring as it is about the reflection. Crisp bright highlights are necessary to illustrate the reflective surfaces of these fabrics.

Step 1: Base color with lightest shade (C3). Leave highlights uncolored.

Step 2: Add shading with medium color (C5).

Step 3: Add deeper shading with dark color (C9).

Step 4: Blend colors together. Leave highlights white. Keep the edge between the light and the highlight crisp.

For a touch more reflection, add a bit of Opaque White to the highlighted area.

Sheer

Sheer fabric is unique in that the under-layers of clothing are visible. Coloring sheer fabric sounds difficult, but it's really just a matter of thinking in layers. Here is a demonstration of coloring a white or silver sheer top.

Step 1: Base color everything that is affected by the sheer fabric. Pay particular attention to the edges. Notice how areas under the sheer fabric are left with white edges.

Notice that the entire dress and both full arms are colored, not just the parts that are under the sheer top.

Step 2: Color and shade those areas affected by the sheer fabric as normal. Make sure to leave edges of areas white.

Step 3: Using the Colorless Blender, lighten the area of the dress and arms lying under the sheer top. **Note:** *Be careful not to push the color into the white edges.*

Remember to color in the direction of the folds.

Step 4: Begin identifying shading in the sheer top with a very light gray (C1). Shading would be in areas that fold and along the edges.

Step 5: Darken the deepest folds with a darker gray (C3). Do not blend.

Tips & Tricks for Coloring Clothing

- *Pleats and fabric folds can appear horizontally or vertically. Always color in the direction of the fold.*

- *Keep the type of fabric in mind before beginning to color.*

- *Make sure the chosen pattern complements the image.*

Because this sheer fabric is clear or a very light white or silver, the color of the object underneath is muted. If the sheer fabric has a tint of color, that will also affect the color of the underlying clothing.

The image below shows the sheer fabric with a hint of turquoise color (BG02), the same color as the dress. Notice how the dress under the sheer top is a touch darker in color. This is because there are two layers of the same color. Notice too how the arms are not darker, but have a slight layer of turquoise over them.

Patterns

Patterns can take fabric from drab to fab! Most often we see colored images wearing solid clothing, but in real life many of us (myself included) gravitate toward prints and patterns. Whether they are bold and bright or soft and subtle, patterns and prints can take your coloring to a whole new level.

Pattern Placement

As long as you follow one simple rule, it's not difficult to create and color patterns.

The Rule

People are not flat; they have dimension, therefore any patterns should have dimension too.

Check out the plaid pattern on the man's shirt in the photo below.

Notice how the lines are completely parallel and perfectly straight. This is not realistic and ends up looking more like grid paper than patterned clothing.

Now look at the plaid pattern on the shirt below.

Notice how the horizontal lines curve slightly? This is because the torso is a cylinder and the lines actually wrap around the body. Also notice how the sleeves are separate sections. This is key to creating realistic patterns.

Another thing to be aware of when coloring patterns on clothing is that clothing can stretch around an object, causing the pattern to stretch also. Take a look at this next photo.

It's the same man, just slightly huskier. Notice how the lines have a more pronounced curve and stretch out as the fabric stretches.

If you have difficulty visualizing how a pattern would look on a body, break it down to basic shapes, find the correct placement and apply it to your image.

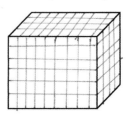

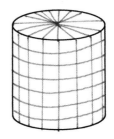

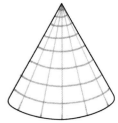

How to Apply Patterns to Clothing

Once you understand the basic concept of how patterns look on a body, it's just a matter of getting out your markers and Multiliners and coloring. Let's walk through coloring a plaid shirt.

Plaid

Step 1: Stamp the image twice. Place one image aside.

Step 2: Base color the shirt with a light color (B21). Dry completely.

Step 3: Using a different-color marker (G14), draw in thick plaid lines.

Start and end your lines outside of the image. This helps to create solid, fully formed lines all the way across the shirt.

Step 4: Using a coordinating-color Multiliner (cobalt .3), draw in thin plaid lines.

Step 5: Cut out the shirt.

Step 6: Color the second image as normal, leaving the shirt uncolored.

Step 7: Adhere shirt to the image.

Encountering Wrinkles

Adding structured patterns to wrinkly clothing is one of the most difficult coloring feats.

Step 1: Color the image as normal. Include any pleats, wrinkles or fabric folds (RV52, RV63, RV55, RV66).

Step 2: Add your pattern. Pay attention to the way the fabric folds.

The areas by the knees that are highlighted are folds that bulge out and the darker shadow areas are places where the fabric tucks in. When adding pattern, follow those movements. Curve out with the bulges and bend in with the tucks. Start with a simple pattern (like stripes) until you feel comfortable with the concept.

Pattern Samples

There are literally thousands of different patterns. Some are structured like stripes and plaids, and some are abstract like flowers or camouflage. To avoid using the same pattern over and over again, start your own collection of patterns and textures.

Print the chart onto your favorite cardstock and start collecting samples of your favorite patterns. Find patterns and textures you like in magazines, on fabric or in photos.

One option is to cut out a small sample of the pattern and adhere it to your pattern chart. This is a great way to collect ideas and build a wonderful pattern sample library.

A more applicable way of using the chart is to take your favorite patterns from magazines, photos and fabric and recreate them using your Copic markers. Attach the colored sample to the blank pattern chart with notes about how the pattern was created. When you want to color clothing and add pattern, just flip through your pattern charts to quickly and easily recreate the look.

Here is a sample page from my pattern collection. Included are animal prints, stripes, random patterns, dots, checks and plaids. I can easily adapt the colors to fit my image.

Included on the CD is a blank patterns chart.

Putting It All *Together*

Now that we've covered how to color skin, hair and clothing, let's walk through the full coloring process for a couple of different images.

Young Girl With Book

Take this opportunity to add texture and pattern to this young schoolgirl image.

Step 1: Base the sweater with R22.

Step 2: Add mid-tone to shaded areas with R24.

Step 3: Add dark shading to sweater with R29.

Step 4: Blend well.

Step 5: Dampen a rag with Colorless Blender solution and place over colored sweater. Do not press or squeeze. Remove the rag to reveal the texture. Let dry completely before moving to Step 6.

Step 6: Base all skin areas with E00.

Step 7: Add mid-tone to shaded areas with E21.

Step 8: Add dark shading to skin with E34.

Step 9: Blend gently and let dry completely before moving to step 10.

Step 10: Add cast shadows to skin with BV02.

Step 11: Base hair with Y23. Let dry completely.

Step 12: Add flicks of Y26 to hair. Do not blend. Let dry completely.

Step 13: Darken hair with flicks of E23. Do not blend.

Step 14: Base skirt with B41.

Step 15: Add shading to skirt with B45.

Step 16: Blend well.

Step 17: Add darkest shading and cast shadows to skirt with B97.

Step 18: Add thin plaid lines to skirt with Cobalt Multiliner.

Step 19: Shade socks with C3.

Step 20: Color and blend shoes with C9, C7 and C5.

Step 21: Color and blend book with G21, G24 and G16.

Old Man With Squirrel

There are lots of opportunities to add texture and pattern to this image. Here we show the basics to get you started.

Step 1: Base sweater with YG61.

Step 2: Feather YG63 on sweater to create shading.

Step 3: Add YG67 to deepest shadows and blend.

Step 4: Let sweater dry completely and add texture with a rag dampened with Colorless Blender.

Step 5: Base skin with E000 and add E70 to shade.

Step 6: Add E43 and E11 to skin for deepest shading. Blend slightly.

Step 7: Add BV20 to shadows of shirt and hair.

Step 8: Color pants with T2, T4 and T6. Add T2 to shadows in hair.

Step 9: Color cane and shoes with E23, E27 and E29.

Step 10: Color squirrel with E23 and E27. Blend and add texture.

Check out Copic Coloring Guide Level 2: Nature for a tutorial on coloring fur!

Little Boy With Ball

Skin tone is very important on this image. It is a young child, so make sure to keep the skin smooth and glowing.

Step 1: Base skin with YR000.

Step 2: Add E11 to shading on skin.

Step 3: Add E13 to shading on skin.

Step 4: Add BV11 to shading on skin and blend slightly.

Step 5: Base hair and ball with Y11.

Step 6: Add Y15 to ball as shadow. Let base color dry on hair and then add flicks of Y15 to shade hair.

Step 7: Shade ball with E11 and blend. Add flicks of E11 and E13 to hair.

Step 8: Base sweater and shoes with R37.

Step 9: Add R59 for shading and blend slightly.

Step 10: Base overalls with B91. While still wet, add in B95 and blend.

Step 11: Add B95 and B99 for shading. Blend slightly.

If you want to add texture to the sweater, color that area and add texture first. Feel free to define the folds and wrinkles in the pants more if wanted.

BONUS
CD
INCLUDED!

Instructions to
complete your cards
are included here!

I ♥ Coloring

Creative Coloring
Projects

Flora's Thoughts

Design by **Colleen Schaan**

Techniques Used
- Coloring Skin
- Coloring Hair
- Coloring Fabric & Clothing

Coloring Instructions

1. Print image onto white smooth cardstock.

2. Color skin with E0000, E01, E21 and a slight bit of E04; blend well.

3. Color lips with E93 and E95.

4. Color eyes with B12 and B26.

5. Color dress with R81, R83, R85 and R89. Add deepest shadows with RV69.

6. Color hair with flicks of YR20, Y21, YR21 and E31. Add fine detail with Multiliner.

7. Color shoes with C7, C5, C3, C1 and C00. ❧

Sources: X-Press It Blending Card, markers, Multiliner, airbrush system, double-sided tape and foam tape from Imagination International Inc.; colored cardstock from Bazzill Basics Paper Inc.; patterned papers from BasicGrey; digital stamp from Sugar Nellie; stamp set from Verve Stamps; Memento ink pad from Imagine Crafts/Tsukineko; pearl flourish from Prima Marketing Inc.; die templates and die-cutting machine from Spellbinders™ Paper Arts.

Materials
Cardstock: white smooth, light yellow, maroon
Lemonade patterned papers: Dandelion, Pretty Petals
Stamps: Flora digital, Wordy Birds set
Dark pink dye ink pad
Markers: B12, B26, C00, C1, C3, C5, C7, E0000, E01, E04, E21, E31, E93, E95, R81, R83, R85, R89, RV69, Y21, YR20, YR21, YR30
Sepia Multiliner
White self-adhesive pearl flourish
Die templates: Labels Eighteen (#S4-310), Labels Four (#S4-190), Fleur De Lis Rectangles (#S4-317)
Grand Calibur®
Airbrush system
Adhesive foam tape
Double-sided tape
Computer with printer

Materials

Cardstock: white smooth, black
Clementine patterned papers: Ivy, Lucy
Stamps: Nevaeh digital, Handmade
    Letters Seals set
Black dye ink pad
Markers: B21, B23, B26, B29, BV20, C0, C1,
    C3, C5, C7, C10, E000, E00, E01, E33,
    R20, W3, W5, W7, Y21, Y23, YG00, YG01,
    YR30, YR31
Colorless Blender (0)
18 inches 1-inch-wide yellow organdy
    ribbon
White string
White/clear flower button
Self-adhesive rhinestone flourish
Die templates: Grand Labels Twenty-
    Three (#LF-347), Petite Oval SM (#S4-
    140), Lace Doily Accents (#S5-062),
    desired Scalloped Oval
Grand Calibur®
Sewing machine with white thread
Adhesive foam squares
Double-sided adhesive
Computer with printer

Because You're Special

Design by Beate Johns

Techniques Used

- Coloring Skin
- Coloring Hair
- Coloring Fabric & Clothing

Coloring Instructions

1. Print image onto white smooth cardstock.

2. Color skin with E000, E00 and E01. Add a cast shadow with BV20.

3. Add blush to cheeks with R20. Blend edges into the skin tone.

4. Color hair with flicks of Y21, Y23 and E33. Let dry before applying next color. Do not blend.

5. Color dress with B21, B23, B26 and B29.

6. Color shoes and waistband with C3, C5, C7 and C10.

7. Color stockings, bottom of shoe and underskirt with C0, C1 and C3.

8. Color eyes with B21 and B23.

9. Create a ground by flicking W3, W5 and W7.

10. Color background by flicking YR30 and YR31 away from image. Soften edges by flicking from outside toward edges with Colorless Blender.

11. To add interest and texture, add dots of varying sizes of YR30, YR31, YG00 and YG01. ✍

Sources: *Cardstock from Neenah Paper Inc.; patterned papers from Cosmo Cricket; digital stamp from Saturated Canary; stamp set from Whimsy Stamps; Memento ink pad from Imagine Crafts/Tsukineko; markers and Colorless Blender from Imagination International Inc.; ribbon from May Arts; rhinestone flourish from Want2Scrap; die templates and die-cutting machine from Spellbinders™ Paper Arts; foam squares from Stampin' Up!; double-sided adhesive from Scor-Pal.*

You Are Loved

Design by **Jennifer Dove**

Techniques Used

- Coloring Skin
- Coloring Hair
- Coloring Fabric & Clothing

Coloring Instructions

1. Merge digital images and print onto white smooth cardstock. Print an additional flower image onto white smooth cardstock.

2. Color skin with E50, E51; blend well. Add cast shadow with E04; do not blend.

3. Color hair with E31, E35, E57 and E79; blend very slightly for a soft look.

4. Color shirt with E31, E35, E57 and E79. Pay attention to fabric folds.

5. Color wings with E50, B32 and YG11. Feather brown into green and green into blue.

6. Add cast shadows from hair onto wings using N3.

7. Color flowers with B32 and B37; blend slightly. Add cast shadows with B39.

8. Color leaves with YG25, YG63, YG95, YG67 and YG99. Add cast shadows with G99.

9. Color flower centers with dots of YR24, E35 and E79.

10. Trim image to 3½ x 5⅜ inches.

11. Airbrush edges with B32. ❧

Sources: *Dark brown cardstock from Bazzill Basics Paper Inc.; paper pad from Graphic 45; digital stamps from Make It Crafty; stamp set from Stampendous! Inc.; black Memento ink pad from Imagine Crafts/Tsukineko; distress ink pad from Ranger Industries Inc.; markers and airbrush system from Imagination International Inc.; pearls from Creative Impressions Inc.; punch from Stampin' Up!; score board from Martha Stewart Crafts; double-sided tape from 3M.*

Materials

Cardstock: white smooth, dark brown
Playtime Past paper pad
Stamps: Fairy Poinsettia digital, Sitting Flower digital, Sincere Sentiment set
Dye ink pads: black, dark brown distress
Markers: B32, B37, B39, E04, E31, E35, E50, E51, E57, E79, G99, N3, YG11, YG25, YG63, YG67, YG95, YG99, YR24
Taupe self-adhesive pearls
Ticket corner punch
Score board
Craft knife
Paper cutter
Blending tool
Airbrush system
Paper adhesive
Double-sided tape

I'm so sorry...

KNOW THAT YOU ARE LOVED

Materials

Cardstock: dark blue, yellow, red, white smooth
Patterned papers: Lost and Found 2 Breeze Dream Wallpaper, blue/yellow dot
On the Pot boy C digital stamp
Dark brown distress ink pad
Markers: 110, B34, B37, B39, E23, E27, E29, E31, E40, E41, E42, E43, E44, E47, E49, E57, E79, N4, N7, R35, R46, R59, YR23, W1, W3, W5, W7, W9
Colorless Blender refill (0)
Multiliner
Burlap
Rag
Airbrush system
Adhesive foam tape
Repositionable tape
Double-sided adhesive
Computer with printer

Succeed

Design by **Jennifer Dove**

Techniques Used
- Coloring Skin
- Coloring Hair
- Coloring Fabric & Clothing

Coloring Instructions

1. Print image onto white smooth cardstock. Trim to 3⅝ x 4⅛ inches.

2. Color shirt with B34, B37 and B39.

3. Dampen a rag with Colorless Blender and hold down over colored shirt. Remove to reveal texture.

4. Add cast shadows on shirt with N7.

5. Print second image onto scrap paper and cut out to create a mask. Attach mask over stamped image using repositionable tape.

6. Airbrush background with E31.

7. Dampen burlap with Colorless Blender and hold down over airbrushed background. Remove to reveal texture. Remove mask.

8. Color skin with E23, E27 and E29.

9. Color hair with squiggles of E44, E79, E49 and 110. Do not blend.

10. Color potty with E40, E41, E42, E4 and E44. Add cast shadows with E47.

11. Shade ground with W1 and E57.

12. Color socks with W1, W3, W5, W7 and W9.

13. Color heel and toe of socks with R35, R46 and R59.

14. Color book with YR23, N4, R35 and E31. 🐾

Sources: Colored cardstock from Bazzill Basics Paper Inc.; Dream Wallpaper patterned paper from My Mind's Eye; digital image from Mo's Digital Pencil; ink pad from Ranger Industries Inc.; markers, Multiliner, Colorless Blender refill and airbrush system from Imagination International Inc.; double-sided adhesive from 3M.

Your Time to Shine

Design by **Colleen Schaan**

Techniques Used

- Coloring Skin
- Coloring Hair
- Coloring Fabric & Clothing

Coloring Instructions

1. Stamp image onto white smooth cardstock.

2. Color skin with E0000, E40, E42, E70 and E71. Blend in E01 at cheekbone. Add cast shadows to skin with V20.

3. Color hair with flicks of E21, E23, E25, E27 and E29; blend slightly.

4. Color eyes with B12 and B26.

5. Color lips with E93 and R85.

6. Color armor with V20, V22, V25 and V28; blend well.

7. Color shirt and bow with C1, C3 and C5. Blend to white with Colorless Blender.

8. Color trim with Y11, Y35 and Y26. Add lemon and gold glitter pen.

9. Color background by flicking with BG70 and BG72. Start near image and flick outward. Blend to white with Colorless Blender. ☙

Sources: X-Press It Blending Card, markers, glitter pen, foam tape and double-sided tape from Imagination International Inc.; colored cardstock from Bazzill Basics Paper Inc.; patterned paper from Lily Bee Design; stamp from Sweet Pea Stamps; stamp set from Verve Stamps; Memento ink pad from Imagine Crafts/Tsukineko; ribbon from The Ribbon Boutique; die templates and die-cutting machine from Spellbinders™ Paper Arts.

Materials

Cardstock: white smooth, lavender, light aqua, aqua
Picket Fence Veranda patterned paper
Stamps: Meredith Dillman's Sheet 2 (Plate 87), Starlight Starbright set
Black dye ink pad
Markers: B12, B26, BG70, BG72, C1, C3, C5, E0000, E01, E21, E23, E25, E27, E29, E40, E42, E70, E71, E93, R85, V20, V22, V25, V28, Y11, Y26, Y35
Colorless Blender (0)
Glitter pens: gold, lemon
White satin ribbon: 16½ inches ⅝-inch-wide, 6 inches ⅛-inch-wide
Hat pin
Labels Eighteen die templates (#S4-310)
Grand Calibur®
Adhesive foam tape
Double-sided tape

Silver Fairy

Design by **Beate Johns**

Techniques Used

- Coloring Skin
- Coloring Hair
- Coloring Fabric & Clothing

Coloring Instructions

1. Stamp image onto white smooth cardstock.

2. Color skin with E000, E01 and E11. Add a cast shadow with BV00.

3. Color hair with flicks of C3, C5, C7 and C10. Let each layer dry before applying next color; do not blend.

4. Color dress with G20, G21 and G24.

5. Color yellow flowers with Y15 and Y17.

6. Color red flowers with R29 and E35.

7. Color bell with Y35, Y38 and E35.

8. Color wings by flicking YR30 into Y21 and G20 into G21. Flick YR30 from opposite side of green parts of wing to give them a yellow hue.

9. For texture, add small dots to wings with YR30, Y21, G20 and G21.

10. To give wings a soft shimmer, color over yellow parts with buttermilk glitter pen; color over green parts with clear glitter pen.

11. Draw blades of grass with YG17.

12. To create ground, add dots of varying sizes of YG17, YG13, YG11, E31 and E30. ♣

Sources: Cardstock from Neenah Paper Inc.; Designer Paper Pad from My Mind's Eye; stamps from Whimsy Stamps; Memento ink pad from Imagine Crafts/ Tsukineko; markers, glitter pen and airbrush system from Imagination International Inc.; rhinestone flourish from Want2Scrap; ribbon from May Arts; Cloud Trio dies from My Favorite Things; die templates and die-cutting machine from Spellbinders™ Paper Arts; corner rounder punch from We R Memory Keepers; Eclipse art masking tape from JudiKins Inc.; foam dots from Stampin' Up!; double-sided adhesive from Scor-Pal.

Materials

Cardstock: white smooth, black, kraft
Lost & Found 2 Rosy 6 x 6 Designer Paper Pad
Stamps: Silver Fairy, Magical Mini Letter Seals
Black dye ink pad
Markers: B02, BV00, C3, C5, C7, C10, E000, E01, E11, E30, E31, E35, R22, R29, G20, G21, G24, W0, W2, Y15, Y17, Y21, Y35, Y38, YG11, YG13, YG17, YR30
Glitter pens: clear, buttermilk
Silver self-adhesive rhinestone flourish
21 inches 1-inch-wide red organdy ribbon
Die templates: Cloud Trio (#MFCL0410), Grand Scalloped Circles (#LF-124), Grand Circles (#LF-114), Standard Circles LG (#S4-114)
Grand Calibur®
Sewing machine
Corner rounder punch
Airbrush system
Art masking tape
Adhesive foam dots
Double-sided adhesive

First Kiss

Design by **Jane Allen**

Techniques Used

- Coloring Skin
- Coloring Hair
- Coloring Fabric & Clothing

Coloring Instructions

1. Print digital image onto white smooth cardstock.

2. Using a Multiliner, draw a line to indicate floor and wall; trim to 4 x 4½ inches.

3. Color wall area evenly with YR30.

4. Dab colored area with a sponge that has been sprayed with Colorless Blender to give a spotty appearance.

5. Add dots of E81, G20 and YG91 randomly over this area repeating sponge technique as necessary.

6. Color floor with E40.

7. Spray Colorless Blender solution onto a piece of 18-count Aida fabric and carefully lay fabric onto floor area for a count of three giving floor a subtle texture.

8. Add shadows to floor using E81, E87, W00, W1, W3 and YG91.

9. Color skin with E0000, E000, E00, E04, E21, W2, W3 and W4.

10. Color lips with R11 and R12.

11. Color hair with flicks of E50, E51, E55, E57 and E59. Do not blend.

12. Color boy's sweater with BG93, BG96 and BG99.

13. Using a Multiliner, draw diamonds on body of sweater. Lighten centers with Colorless Blender.

14. Color boy's jeans with B91, B93, B95, B97, N3 and N5. Highlight seams with Colorless Blender.

15. Color boy's shoes with BG70, BG72, BG75, BG78 and G94.

16. Color rubber on shoes with B000, W00, W0, W1, W2 and W7.

17. Color flowers with E04, E07, E53, E55 and E81.

18. Color boy's shirt with B0000, W0, W1, W2 and W3.

19. Color girl's sweater with E53, E55, W4, W6 and W7.

20. Color hair bows and skirt with E11, E13, E15, E17, E18, W4, W6 and E49.

21. Color socks with E50, E51, W1 and W2.

22. Color girl's shoes with B0000, W00, W0, W1, W2, W3 and G85, G94 and YG91. 🐾

Sources: White smooth cardstock from Personal Impressions; colored cardstock from Craft Creations; paper pack from Do Crafts; digital stamp from Make It Crafty; markers and Multiliner from Imagination International Inc.; permanent transfer tape pen from Stix2; chalk ink pad from Imagine Crafts/Tsukineko; ribbon from We R Memory Keepers.

Materials

Cardstock: white smooth, dark brown, brown
Papermania Hampstead paper pack
Geeky Love digital stamp
Brown chalk ink pad
Markers: B0000, B000, B91, B93, B95, B97, BG70, BG72, BG75, BG78, BG93, BG96, BG99, E0000, E000, E00, E04, E07, E11, E13, E15, E17, E18, E21, E40, E49, E50, E51, E53, E55, E57, E59, E81, E87, G20, G85, G94, N3, N5, R11, R12, W00, W0, W1, W2, W3, W4, W6, W7, YG91, YR30
Colorless Blender refill (0)
Black Multiliner
8 inches ⅜-inch-wide orange/green striped ribbon
18-count Aida fabric (cross-stitch fabric)
Spray bottle
Natural sponge
Adhesive pen
Computer with printer

Peeking

Design by **Melissa Andrew**

Techniques Used
- Coloring Skin
- Coloring Hair
- Coloring Fabric & Clothing

Coloring Instructions

1. Print image onto white smooth cardstock.

2. Color skin with E000, E00 and E11. Add cast shadow with BV00.

3. Add cheeks with R20.

4. Color hair with flicks of E71, E74, E77 and E79; do not blend.

5. Color dress and shirt with R81, R83, R85 and R89.

6. Add dot pattern with Opaque White pigment.

7. Color shoes with R81, R83, R85, R89, W1 and W3.

8. Color tree with E71, E74, E77 and E79.

9. Color bird with B0000, B000, B01 and B02.

10. Color nest with E50, E51, E53 and E55.

11. Color grass and leaves with YG93, YG95 and YG97; do not blend. ❧

Sources: X-Press It Blending Card, markers and Opaque White pigment from Imagination International Inc.; colored cardstock from Bazzill Basics Paper Inc. and Stampin' Up!; patterned papers from My Mind's Eye; digital stamp from Tiddly Inks; die templates from Spellbinders™ Paper Arts; die-cutting machine from Provo Craft; double-sided tape from 3M.

Materials
Cardstock: white smooth, dark brown, green, cream
Lost & Found 2 Blush patterned papers: Favorite Party, Better Dotted
Wryn New Nest digital stamp
Markers: B0000, B000, B01, B02, BV00, E000, E00, E11, E50, E51, E53, E55, E71, E74, E77, E79, R20, R81, R83, R85, R89, W1, W3, YG93, YG95, YG97
Opaque White pigment
Green buttons
Twine: dark brown, light brown
Standard Circles LG die templates (#S4-114)
Die-cutting machine
Paintbrush
Double-sided tape
Computer with printer

Materials

Cardstock: white smooth, light blue, light orange
Copica digital stamp
Brown chalk ink pad
Markers: B41, B45, C1, C3, E000, E13, E21, E31, E33, E35, E41, E42, E43, R20, R24, RV63, RV66, V15, W0, W1, YG61, YG63, YR04, YR21, YR23
Blue button
Nested Lacey Pennants die templates (#S5-029)
Die-cutting machine
Scallop-edged scissors
Sewing machine with white thread
Adhesive foam tape
Paper adhesive
Computer with printer

I Love Coloring!

Design by **Sharon Harnist**

Techniques Used

- Coloring Skin
- Coloring Hair
- Coloring Fabric & Clothing

Coloring Instructions

1. Print digital image twice onto white smooth cardstock. ***Note:*** *Color one full image; color only the heart on remaining image; cut out colored heart.*

2. Color hair with flicks of YR21, E31, E33 and E35; do not blend.

3. Color skin with E000, E21, E13 and E31.

4. Add cheeks and color lips with R20.

5. Color eyes with B41.

6. Color denim jumper and jeans with B41 and B45.

7. Color patch on apron and solid long shirt/dress with YR21 and YR23.

8. Color striped long shirt/dress, heart and hair clips with RV63 and RV66.

9. Color eyelet skirt/slip and apron with E41, E42 and E43.

10. Color marker lids with various colors: C3, V15, R20, R24, RV63, YR21, YR04, YG61, YG63, B41, E13 and E31.

11. Color some marker barrels with C1.

12. Add cast shadows around girl with W0 and W1. ❧

Sources: X-Press It Blending Card, markers and foam tape from Imagination International Inc.; light blue and light orange cardstock from Stampin' Up!; digital stamp from Saturated Canary; chalk ink pad from Clearsnap Inc.; button from Papertrey Ink; die templates and die-cutting machine from Spellbinders™ Paper Arts.

Kisses

Design by **Michelle Houghton**

Techniques Used
- Coloring Skin
- Coloring Hair

Coloring Instructions

1. Print image onto white smooth cardstock.

2. Color boots and dog with E21, E33 and E35; blend well.

3. Color shorts with B91, B95 and B97.

4. Color shirt with YR15, YR16 and YR18.

5. Color skin with E25, E27 and E29. Use E29 sparingly to avoid blurring details.

6. Color collar with BG93 and BG96.

7. Color dog tag with Y26.

8. Color tongue, bandage and fingernails with E04.

9. Add cast shadow on ground with W1.

10. Color hair by drawing squiggles with C3, C5, C7 and C9; do not blend. ✿

Sources: X-Press It Blending Card and markers from Imagination International Inc.; cream cardstock from Bazzill Basics Paper Inc.; patterned papers and fabric paper from American Crafts; digital stamp set from Mo's Digital Pencil; Memento ink pad from Imagine Crafts/ Tsukineko; adhesive dots from Therm O Web; double-sided tape from 3M.

Materials
Cardstock: white smooth, cream
Amy Tangerine patterned papers: Orange You Glad, Yes Peas
Amy Tangerine You're Golden Fabric Paper
Bronte Kisses digital stamp set
Dark brown dye ink pad
Markers: B91, B95, B97, BG93, BG96, C3, C5, C7, C9, E04, E21, E25, E27, E29, E33, E35, W1, Y26, YR15, YR16, YR18
Buttons
Twine
Adhesive dots
Double-sided tape
Computer with printer

Dream Big

Design by Colleen Schaan

Technique Used
• Coloring Skin

Coloring Instructions

1. Print image onto white smooth cardstock.

2. Color skin with E50, E21 and E34; blend slightly. Add cast shadows with BV02.

3. Color hair with E34 and E49. Add a highlight with Colorless Blender.

4. Color red stripes and cuffs with R22, R24 and R39. Keep highlight bright.

5. Color blue stripes and stars with B12 and B26.

6. Ground image with E23.

Sources: X-Press It Blending Card, markers, Multiliner and foam tape from Imagination International Inc.; colored cardstock from Bazzill Basics Paper Inc.; digital stamp from Mo's Digital Pencil; stamp set from Verve Stamps; Memento ink pad from Imagine Crafts/Tsukineko; brads from American Crafts; die templates and die-cutting machine from Spellbinders™ Paper Arts.

Materials
Cardstock: white smooth, blue Dotted Swiss, red
Stamps: Strongman digital, Words of Wisdom set
Black dye ink pad
Markers: B12, B26, BV02, E21, E23, E34, E49, E50, R22, R24, R39
Colorless Blender (0)
Black Multiliner
White brads
Die templates: Standard Circles LG (#S4-114), Standard Circles SM (#S4-116)
Grand Calibur®
Paper piercer
Adhesive foam tape
Double-sided tape
Computer with printer

Asian Thanks

Design by **Claudia Rosa**

Technique Used

- Coloring Skin
- Coloring Hair
- Coloring Fabric & Clothing

Coloring Instructions

1. Stamp image onto a 4½ x 4½-inch piece of white smooth cardstock. Stamp a second image onto a sticky note or masking material.

2. Stamp sentiment in black ink on bottom left side of image.

3. Color ground with E31, E34, W4 and W5. Blend out with W00.

4. Cut out masking image and place over stamped image.

5. Airbrush B000 onto background. Remove mask.

6. Color skirt with RV00, R81 and R85.

7. Color kimono with YG000, G24, YG17 and YG67.

8. Color trim with R81 and B00.

9. Color branch with E27.

10. Color skin with E00, E11 and E21. Add W1 for cast shadows.

11. Color cheeks with R20 and blend into skin tone.

12. Color hair with flicks of C5, C6, C8, C9 and 110. Do not blend.

13. Color shoes with C5, C6, C8 and C9.

14. Color umbrella with RV00, R81 and R85. Add G24 to center and blend.

15. Color handle of umbrella with E34 and E27. ❧

Sources: White smooth X-Press It Blending Card, markers, Colorless Blender and airbrush system from Imagination International Inc.; remaining cardstock from Stampin' Up! and Bazzill Basics Paper Inc.; paper pack and Chinese Tilda stamps from MAGNOLIA-licious; Memento ink pad from Imagine Crafts/Tsukineko; twine and buttons from The Ribbon Girls; paper flowers and leaves from Wild Orchid Crafts; quick-drying paper adhesive from 3M; super tacky glue from iLoveToCreate.

Materials

Cardstock: white smooth, pink, green, white
Winner Takes It All paper pack: Champion Flower in Blue patterned paper
Sticky note or masking material
Stamps: Chinese Tilda, "Thank you"
Black dye ink pad
Markers: 110, B000, B00, C5, C6, C8, C9, E00, E11, E21, E27, E31, E34, G24, R20, R81, R85, RV00, W00, W1, W4, W5, YG000, YG17, YG67
Colorless Blender (0)
White gel pen
Twine
Faceted sparkle buttons
Paper flowers and leaves
Stamp positioner
Airbrush system
Sewing machine with white thread
Glitter glue: iridescent, silver
Adhesive foam tape
3M quick-drying adhesive
Super tacky glue

Materials

Cardstock: white smooth, kraft
Six By Six Blink of an Eye paper pad
Stamps: School Mae digital, Always & Forever set
Black dye ink pad
Markers: BG10, BG11, BG15, BV02, E000, E00, E11, E41, E42, E44, E50, E51, E53, E55, R20, YR00, YR12, YR15, YR18
Opaque White pigment
Die templates: Standard Circles LG (#S4-114), Lacy Circles (#S4-293)
Die-cutting machine
Yellow self-adhesive pearls
Yellow baker's twine
Corner rounder punch
Paintbrush
Adhesive foam tape
Double-sided tape
Computer with printer

Not So Shy

Design by **Melissa Andrew**

Techniques Used

- Coloring Hair
- Coloring Skin
- Coloring Fabric & Clothing

Coloring Instructions

1. Color skin with E000, E00 and E11. Add cast shadows with BV02.

2. Color cheeks with R20.

3. Color hair with flicks of E50, E51, E53 and E55; do not blend.

4. Color shirt, skirt and shoes with E41, E42 and E44.

5. Color sweater and socks with YR00, YR12, YR15 and YR18.

6. Color eyes and book with BG10, BG11 and BG15

7. Add highlights to eyes with Opaque White pigment.

Sources: X-Press It Blending Card, markers and Opaque White pigment from Imagination International Inc.; kraft cardstock from Bazzill Basics Paper Inc.; paper pad from My Mind's Eye; digital stamp from Some Odd Girl; stamp set from My Craft Spot; Memento ink pad from Imagine Crafts/Tsukineko; die templates from Spellbinders™ Paper Arts; foam tape from Michaels Stores Inc.; double-sided tape from 3M.

Together

Design by **Michelle Houghton**

Techniques Used
- Coloring Hair
- Coloring Skin

Coloring Instructions

1. Print image onto white smooth cardstock.

2. Color mother's dress with YR000, R20, R22 and a small amount of R24; blend well.

3. Color girl's dress with YG11 and YG13; blend well.

4. Color skin with YR000 and YR01. Notice sharp shadow on neck.

5. Color mother's hair with flicks of YR30, YR31, YR15, YR18 and E09; do not blend.

6. Color girl's hair with flicks of YR30, YR31, YR14 and YR15; do not blend.

7. Base sky with Colorless Blender. Color sky by flicking B91 from outer edge toward image. Blend with Colorless Blender.

8. Add ground by basing with YG93. Add dots of varying sizes of YG95 and YG97. ❧

Sources: *X-Press It Blending Card, markers and Colorless Blender from Imagination International Inc.; green cardstock from Bazzill Basics Paper Inc.; patterned papers from Graphic 45; digital stamp from A Day For Daisies; alphabet stamp set from Hampton Art; Memento ink pad from Imagine Crafts/Tsukineko; canvas tag from Maya Road; twine from American Crafts; adhesive dots from Therm O Web; double-sided tape from 3M.*

Materials
Cardstock: white smooth, green
Patterned papers: Once Upon a Springtime
    Spellbound, floral
Stamps: Booktime digital, alphabet set
Dark brown dye ink pad
Markers: B91, E09, R20, R22, R24, YG11,
    YG13, YG93, YG95, YG97, YR000, YR01,
    YR14, YR15, YR18, YR30, YR31
Colorless Blender (0)
Twine
Buttons
Canvas tag
Adhesive dots
Double-sided tape
Computer with printer

Love You

Design by **Marianne Walker**

Technique used

- Coloring Skin

Coloring Instructions

1. Stamp image onto white cardstock.

2. Color skin with E000, E01, E11, E04 and E71. Darken shadow areas with B41 and BG70.

3. Color hair with E71, E77 and W9.

4. Color hat and dress with BG70, B000, B41, B93 and B97.

5. Color flowers with E04 and E77.

6. Color leaves with G24 and B97.

7. Place lace into sandwich bag with several drops of E44 ink refill. Squeeze bag to ink lace thoroughly. Remove from bag; let dry. ❧

Sources: *X-Press It Blending Card, markers, foam tape and double-sided tape from Imagination International Inc.; white cardstock from Neenah Paper Inc.; paper pad from GCD Studios Inc.; stamps from Our Craft Lounge; Memento ink pad from Imagine Crafts/Tsukineko; pearls from Kaisercraft.*

Materials

Cardstock: white smooth, white
12 x 12-inch Ella Blue Paper Pad
Vintage Roses stamp set
Black dye ink pad
Markers: B000, B41, B93, B97, BG70, E000, E01, E04, E11, E71, E77, G24, W9
E44 ink refill
White self-adhesive pearls
5 inches 1¼-inch-wide ivory lace
Sandwich bag
Adhesive foam tape
Double-sided tape

Believe

Design by **Jennifer Dove**

Techniques Used
- Coloring Skin
- Coloring Hair
- Coloring Fabric & Clothing

Coloring Instructions

1. Print digital image onto white smooth cardstock and trim to 4 x 4½ inches.

2. Airbrush edges of image with E35 and E31 as shown.

3. Dampen a rag with Colorless Blender and place over airbrushed background. Remove to reveal texture.

4. Color hat with E37, YR24 and E99.

5. Dampen burlap with Colorless Blender and place over colored hat. Remove to reveal texture.

6. Color skin with E50, E51 and E04.

7. Add cheeks with E93; blend into skin tone.

8. Color eyes with YG25 and YG67.

9. Shade eye with N2.

10. Color hair with flicks of E23, E25, E29 and E79.

11. Color jacket with B91, B95, B97 and B99.

12. Color dress with Y00, Y02, Y08 and Y18.

13. Color flowers with E23 and E79. Work your way out from the center with Y15 and R08.

14. Color leaves with YG25 and YG67. ❧

Sources: *Colored cardstock from Bazzill Basics Paper Inc.; patterned papers from Graphic 45; digital image from Sugar Nellie; Believe stamp from Just For Fun Rubber Stamps; Memento ink pad from Imagine Crafts/Tsukineko; markers, Colorless Blender refill and airbrush system from Imagination International Inc.; double-sided adhesive from 3M.*

Materials
Cardstock: white smooth, black, dark brown
Patterned papers: black/text dot, maroon flower, cream/red stripe
Victoria digital stamp
"BELIEVE" stamp
Brown dye ink pad
Markers: B91, B95, B97, B99, E04, E23, E25, E29, E31, E35, E37, E50, E51, E79, E93, E99, N2, R08, Y00, Y02, Y08, Y15, Y18, YG25, YG67, YR24
Colorless Blender refill (0)
Copper nailheads
Burlap
Rag
Airbrush system
Adhesive foam tape
Double-sided adhesive

Materials

Cardstock: white smooth, blue, red
Sasparilla patterned papers: Rustler,
    Dash Dalton
Chocolate Smile digital stamp
Light brown dye ink pad
Markers: BV000, BV01, B41, B45, B47,
    BG000, E000, E00, E11, E31, E33, E37, E59,
    E97, R12, R14, R17, R29, T0, T2, YR31, YR32
Colorless Blender (0)
Colorless Blender refill (0) (optional)
Buttermilk glitter pen
Wooden button
Cotton string
10 inches ¾-inch-wide natural twill tape
Die templates: Splendid Circles (#S4-354),
    Grand Labels Eleven (#LF-246)
Grand Calibur®
Sewing machine with white thread
Sanding block
Scrap of denim fabric (optional)
Adhesive foam tape
Paper adhesive
Computer with printer

Chocolate Fixes Everything!

Design by **Debbie Olson**

Techniques Used

- Coloring Skin
- Coloring Hair
- Coloring Fabric & Clothing

Coloring Instructions

1. Print image onto white smooth cardstock.

2. Color denim with B41, B45 and B47. *Option: If desired, create a denim pattern on overalls by applying Colorless Blender refill to scrap of denim fabric. Place denim fabric onto colored area and lightly press. Remove fabric.*

3. Color skin with E000, E00 and E11. Add cast shadows with BV000.

4. While facial skin tones are still damp, add chocolate around mouth, if desired, using E37 and E59.

5. Color hair with flicks of YR31, YR32 and E97. Use a glitter pen to add a few highlights to hair.

6. Color shirt with R12, R14, R17 and R29.

7. Color chocolate bar with E31, E33, E37 and E59. Add a touch of BV01 to further cool shadows.

8. Shade socks with T0, T2 and BV000, softening with Colorless Blender where desired.

9. Color sock bands with R12, R14 and R29.

10. Add shadows behind legs and to plane on which child is sitting so child does not seem to float.

11. Color background, using flicks of BG000 softened with Colorless Blender. Add in a touch of BV000 on shadow side. ✿

Sources: X-Press It Blending Card, markers, Colorless Blender, glitter pen and foam tape from Imagination International Inc.; colored cardstock from Stampin' Up!; patterned papers from October Afternoon; digital stamp from Mo's Digital Pencil; vintage button from Papertrey Ink; dies and die-cutting machine from Spellbinders™ Paper Arts; paper adhesive from Tombow USA.

Curiouser

Design by **Melanie Holtz**

Techniques Used

- Coloring Hair
- Coloring Skin
- Coloring Fabric & Clothing

Coloring Instructions

1. Stamp images onto white cardstock with black ink.

2. Color Alice's skin with E000, E00 and E11.

3. Add cheeks with R20 and blend into skin tone.

4. Color Alice's hair with flicks of E50, Y21, Y23, E31, E33 and E37. Let ink dry between layers for added texture.

5. Color dress with B32, B34, B37 and BV29.

6. Shade stocking stripes and blouse with C00, C1, C3, C5 and C7.

7. Color Hatter's skin with E000, E00, E11 and RV95. *Tip: Use RV95 sparingly.*

8. Color Hatter's hair with flicks of E50, E31, E33, E37 and E59.

9. Color hat and shirt with BG0000, BG000, BG72, BG75 and BV29.

10. Color tie and hatband with YR31, YR23, Y23, E13, E18 and E99.

11. Color vest with R22, R27, R46, R59 and BV23.

12. Color pants with C1, C3, C5 and C7.

13. Color teacup with C00, C1, C3 and C5 with a bit of E13 for the tea.

Sources: White smooth cardstock from Neenah Paper Inc.; colored cardstock from Bazzill Basics Paper Inc.; patterned papers from My Mind's Eye; stamp sets from Kraftin' Kimmie Stamps; Memento black ink pad and VersaFine ink pad from Imagine Crafts/Tsukineko; distress ink from Ranger Industries Inc.; markers from Imagination International Inc.; die templates from Spellbinders™ Paper Arts; die-cutting machine from Provo Craft; paper adhesive from Tombow USA.

Materials

Cardstock: white smooth, kraft, dark chocolate

Stella and Rose patterned papers: Hazel Fancy Lots of Dots, Hattie Boy Tapestry, Gertie Little One Blooms die cut, Hattie Family Silk Tie die cut

Stamp sets: Alice in Wonderland, Mad Hatter

Dye ink pads: black, fine-detail black, dark brown distress

Markers: B32, B34, B37, BG0000, BG000, BG72, BG75, BV23, BV29, C00, C1, C3, C5, C7, E000, E00, E11, E13, E18, E31, E33, E37, E50, E59, E99, R20, R22, R27, R46, R59, RV95, Y21, Y23, YR23, YR31

Self-adhesive pearls

Die templates: Labels Eight (#S4- 019), Labels Eighteen (#S4-310), Parisian Accents (#S5-034)

Die-cutting machine

Sewing machine with white thread

Paper adhesive

Materials

Cardstock: white smooth, teal, light teal
Swimming Pool Daisy Strips patterned
   paper
Stamps: Bling Baby, Disco Queen set
Black dye ink pad
Markers: BG000, BG02, BG05, BG07, BG49,
   BG70, E08, E13, E21, E30, E31, E33, E35,
   E37, E50, E51, E55, E59, E97, R43, R46,
   G16, YG09
Black Multiliner
Lemon glitter pen
Opaque White pigment
Teal self-adhesive gems
Wonky Rectangles die templates (#S4-306)
Grand Calibur®
Paintbrush
Adhesive foam tape
Double-sided tape

The Flip Side

Design by **Colleen Schaan**

Techniques Used

- Coloring Skin
- Coloring Hair
- Coloring Fabric & Clothing

Coloring Instructions

1. Stamp image onto white cardstock with black ink.

2. Color skin with E30, E33, E35 and E37.

3. Color lips with R43 and R46.

4. Color eyes with YG09 and G16.

5. Color hair by adding dots of E13, E97, E08 and E59; do not blend.

6. Color clothing with BG000, BG02, BG05, BG07 and BG49; blend well.

7. Color boots with flicks of E50, E51, E31 and E55.

8. Add lemon glitter pen over jewelry.

9. Add highlights to glasses with Opaque White pigment.

10. Create background with dots of E50, BG70 and E21. ✿

Sources: *X-Press It Blending Card, markers, Multiliner, glitter pen, Opaque White, foam tape and double-sided tape from Imagination International Inc.; colored cardstock from Bazzill Basics Paper Inc.; patterned paper from Doodlebug Design Inc.; stamp from Whimsy Stamps; stamp set from My Favorite Things; Memento ink pad from Imagine Crafts/Tsukineko; gems from The Paper Studio; die templates and die-cutting machine from Spellbinders™ Paper Arts.*

Style Is Everything

Design by **Colleen Schaan**

Techniques Used
- Coloring Skin
- Coloring Hair
- Coloring Fabric & Clothing

Coloring Instructions

1. Stamp image onto white smooth cardstock.

2. Color man's skin with E50, E21, E53 and E33. Let layers dry a bit between blending.

3. Color woman's skin with E50, E53, E35 and E37. Use only a touch of E37 in shadows.

4. Add cheeks to woman with E93, E95 and RV19. Blend into skin tone.

5. Add lips to woman with RV55 and RV19.

6. Color woman's shirt, headband and leg warmers with RV52, RV55, RV66 and RV09. This is a difficult blend and takes work to get smooth.

7. Color glasses, leggings and bracelets with BG000, BG02 and BG05.

8. Color lenses with C3, C1 and C00.

9. Color both sets of shoes with C7, C3 and C1; blend lightly.

10. Color man's pants with BV20. Add plaid with wide stripes of BV25 and thin stripes of sky blue Multiliner.

11. Color man's shirt with B00, B12 and B14; blend well.

12. Color hair with flicks of BV20 and C3; do not blend.

13. Color belt buckle with Y23 and Y17.

14. Add ground with C1, C3 and C5. 🎨

Sources: X-Press It Blending Card, markers, Multiliner, foam tape and double-sided tape from Imagination International Inc.; colored cardstock from Bazzill Basics Paper Inc.; stamp set from Art Impressions Inc.; Memento ink pad from Imagine Crafts/Tsukineko; punches from Stampin' Up!

Materials
Cardstock: white smooth, dark pink, pink
    Dotted Swiss, turquoise, light turquoise
80s stamp set
Black dye ink pad
Markers: B00, B12, B14, BG000, BG02, BG05,
    BV20, BV25, C00, C1, C3, C5, C7, E21, E33,
    E35, E37, E50, E53, E93, E95, RV09, RV19,
    RV52, RV55, RV66, Y17, Y23
Multiliner: black, sky blue
Circle punches: 1³⁄₈-inch, 1¹⁄₄-inch
Adhesive foam tape
Double-sided tape

Happy Unbirthday to YOU!

Design by **Michele Boyer**

Techniques Used

- Coloring Skin
- Coloring Hair
- Coloring Fabric & Clothing

Coloring Instructions

1. Stamp image onto white cardstock.

2. Using BG70, add shadow around image. Soften edges using Colorless Blender.

3. Color skin with E000, E00 and E11; blend gently.

4. Color cheeks using R20. Blend edges into skin tone.

5. Shade eyes with B000.

6. Color hair with flicks of Y21, YR24, E35 and E37; do not blend.

7. Color dress and hair bow with B91, B93, B95 and B97.

8. Shade slip with E41.

9. Color dress bow with Y21 and YR24.

10. Color stockings with B93 and YR24 leaving upper edges white.

11. Shade stockings with W00 and W3.

12. Color shoes with B97.

13. Place ribbon in a sandwich bag and add several drops of W7 ink refill. Squeeze bag to ink ribbon thoroughly. Remove from bag; let dry. ✿

Sources: X-Press It Blending Card, markers and Colorless Blender from Imagination International Inc.; colored cardstock by Papertrey Ink; patterned papers by October Afternoon; stamps from Kraftin' Kimmie Stamps; Memento ink pad from Imagine Crafts/Tsukineko; ribbon from Stampin' Up!; die templates from Spellbinders™ Paper Arts; circle cutter from Creative Memories.

Cowboy Birthday

Design by Colleen Schaan

Techniques Used

- Coloring Skin
- Coloring Fabric & Clothing

Coloring Instructions

1. Stamp image onto white cardstock with dark brown ink.

2. Color skin with E40, E70 and E04. Add E23 for beard.

3. Color chaps, vest and gloves with Y23, E81, E84 and E34; blend well.

4. Color gun with C3 and C7.

5. Color boots, hat and belt with E55, E57 and E59; blend well.

6. Color shirt with R22, R27 and R46. Add narrow plaid stripes with wine Multiliner.

7. Color buckle and spurs with Y11 and Y35.

8. Color jeans and bandana with B91, B93, B95 and B97.

9. Add ground with E30 and E33. ✒

Sources: X-Press It Blending Card, markers, Multiliner, double-sided tape and foam tape from Imagination International Inc.; colored cardstock from Bazzill Basics Paper Inc.; This End Up patterned paper from 7gypsies; Al Fresco patterned paper from Lily Bee Design; stamps from Art Impressions Inc.; Memento ink pad from Imagine Crafts/Tsukineko; distress dye ink pads from Ranger Industries Inc.; hemp cord from Canvas Corp.; die from My Favorite Things; die-cutting machine from Sizzix.

Materials

Cardstock: white smooth, brown Dotted Swiss, dark brown
Patterned papers: Picket Fence Al Fresco, Postale This End Up
Stamps: Slim, Here's Hopin'
Dye ink pads: dark brown, light brown distress, dark brown distress
Markers: B91, B93, B95, B97, C3, C7, E04, E23, E30, E33, E34, E40, E55, E57, E59, E70, E81, E84, R22, R27, R46, Y11, Y23, Y35
Wine Multiliner
Hemp cord
File Tab die
Die-cutting machine
Paper piercer
Adhesive foam tape
Double-sided tape

Contributors

About the Authors

Colleen Schaan is a Regional Copic Certification Instructor and team member of the Education program in North America and travels extensively across the nation for workshops, demos and trade shows. She holds English and secondary education degrees from Wartburg College and taught English at the middle school, high school and college level for 12 years before retiring to focus on a career in creative arts. She is a co-author of the *Copic Coloring Guide* series and author of a number of Copic technique articles for *CardMaker* magazine. She currently resides in Atlanta, Ga., with her husband and three pets.

Marianne Walker is the Product Director for Imagination International Inc., where she develops product publications and certification manuals. She is a freelance illustrator and Lead Illustrator for Our Craft Lounge. She is the author of *Shadows & Shading: A Beginner's Guide to Lighting Placement* and co-author of the *Copic Coloring Guide* series. She travels throughout the United States teaching drawing and coloring classes at trade shows, stores and art schools. She graduated from the University of Oregon with a bachelor of fine arts in multimedia design and a minor in journalism/advertising. She currently resides in Springfield, Ore., with her husband and two children.

Buyer's Guide

3M
(800) 328-6276
www.scotchbrand.com

7gypsies
(866) 376-9961
www.sevengypsies.com

A Day For Daisies
www.adayfordaisies.com

American Crafts
(801) 226-0747
www.americancrafts.com

Art Impressions Inc.
(800) 393-2014
www.artimpressions.com

Bazzill Basics Paper Inc.
(800) 560-1610
www.bazzillbasics.com

Canvas Corp.
(866) 376-9961
www.canvascorp.com

Clearsnap Inc.
(800) 448-4862
www.clearsnap.com

Cosmo Cricket
(904) 482-0091
www.cosmocricket.com

Craft Creations
www.craftcreations.com

Creative Impressions Inc.
(719) 596-4860
www.creativeimpressions.com

Creative Memories
www.creativememories.com

Do Crafts
www.docrafts.com

Doodlebug Design Inc.
(877) 800-9190
www.doodlebug.ws

GCD Studios Inc.
(877) 272-0262
www.gcdstudios.com

Graphic 45
(866) 573-4806
www.g45papers.com

Hampton Art
(800) 981-5169
www.hamptonart.com

iLoveToCreate™
(800) 438-6226
www.ilovetocreate.com

Imagination International Inc.
(541) 684-0013
www.copicmarker.com

Imagine Crafts/Tsukineko
(425) 883-7733
www.imaginecrafts.com

JudiKins Inc.
(310) 515-1115
www.judikins.com

Just For Fun Rubber Stamps
(727) 376-6289
www.jffstamps.com

Kaisercraft
(888) 684-7147
www.kaisercraft.com

Kraftin' Kimmie Stamps
www.kraftinkimmiestamps.com

Lily Bee Design
(801) 820-6845
www.lilybeedesign.com

MAGNOLIA-licious
(604) 594-5188
www.magnoliastamps.us

Make It Crafty
www.makeitcrafty.com

Martha Stewart Crafts
www.eksuccessbrands.com/
marthastewartcrafts

Maya Road
(877) 427-7764
www.mayaroad.com

May Arts
(203) 637-8366
www.mayarts.com

Michaels Stores Inc.
(800) MICHAELS (642-4235)
www.michaels.com

Mo's Digital Pencil
www.mosdigitalpencil.com

My Craft Spot
http://craftspotbykimberly.
blogspot.com

My Favorite Things
www.mftstamps.com

My Mind's Eye
(800) 665-5116
www.mymindseye.com

Neenah Paper Inc.
(800) 994-5993
www.neenahpaper.com

October Afternoon
(866) 513-5553
www.octoberafternoon.com

Our Craft Lounge
(877) 445-6864
www.ourcraftlounge.net

The Paper Studio
(480) 557-5700
www.paperstudio.com

Papertrey Ink
www.papertreyink.com

Personal Impressions
http://personalimpressions.com

Provo Craft
(800) 937-7686
www.provocraft.com

Ranger Industries Inc.
(732) 389-3535
www.rangerink.com

The Ribbon Boutique
www.theribbonboutique.com

The Ribbon Girls
www.ribbongirl.co.uk

Saturated Canary
http://saturated-canary.myshopify.
com

Scor-Pal Products
(877) 629-9908
www.scor-pal.com

Sizzix
(877) 355-4766
www.sizzix.com

Some Odd Girl
www.someoddgirl.com

Spellbinders™ Paper Arts
(888) 547-0400
www.spellbinderspaperarts.com

Stampendous! Inc.
(800) 869-0474
www.stampendous.com

Stampin' Up!
(800) STAMP UP (782-6787)
www.stampinup.com

Stix2
www.stix2.co.uk

Studio Calico
www.studiocalico.com

Sugar Nellie
www.sugarnellie.com

Sweet Pea Stamps
www.sweetpeastamps.com

Therm O Web Inc.
(800) 323-0799
www.thermowebonline.com

Tiddly Inks
www.tiddlyinks.com

Tombow USA
www.tombowusa.com

Verve Stamps
www.shopverve.com

Want2Scrap
(260) 740-2976
www.want2scrap.com

We R Memory Keepers
(877) PICKWER (742-5937)
www.weronthenet.com

Whimsy Stamps
http://whimsystamps.com

Wild Orchid Crafts
www.wildorchidcrafts.com

The Buyer's Guide listings are provided as a service to our readers and should not be considered an endorsement from this publication.